Praise for previous editions of

CAMPFIRE SONGS

"It never fails. You're seated around the campfire, and someone suggests a sing-along. But somehow, people forget words or, even worse, can't think of a song to sing. It looks as though you need *Campfire Songs.*"

— *Discovery* magazine

"It is a rare person who does not enjoy joining in around a campfire and lifting his or her voice in song. Often the problem is that we do not know all the words to many of the old favorites. That's where this little volume comes to the rescue."

— *Easy Rider,* Dining and Entertainment Guide

"Handy for carrying along to the campfires."

— *Northeast Outdoors*

"Contains more than 100 songs, including folk songs, ballads, spirituals, work songs, rounds, and more. Each entry is musically scored and features guitar chords."

— *National Outdoor Outfitters News*

"A collection of songs to sing—the traditional favorites that people always turn to for informal sing-alongs"

— *Pacific Pipeline*

W9-BCS-359

CAMPFIRE SONGS

THIRD EDITION

Edited by

IRENE MADDOX
and
ROSALYN COBB

The Globe Pequot Press

GUILFORD, CONNECTICUT

To my husband, Robert, with many thanks
for all his help and support with this book.
— Irene Maddox

To all my students,
who continue to teach me so much about life.
— Rosalyn Cobb

To buy books in quantity for corporate use
or incentives, call **(800) 962–0973**
or e-mail **premiums@GlobePequot.com.**

Editorial services provided by Sally Hill McMillan and Associates, Inc.
Music set by Keith Ericksen
Cover design and photography by Schwartzman Design

ISBN: 978-0-7627-0318-0

Manufactured in the United States of America
Third Edition/Ninth Printing

Contents

American Folk Songs and Rounds

Patriotic Songs

Introduction

Singing around a campfire or fireplace has been a natural and enjoyable way to close a day of hiking, camping, or work for centuries. Since recorded history began, we know that singing has been a major entertainment for many people.

Many songs have been passed down from one generation to another. Melodies have been altered to fit the singer or the place, but the spirit of the music lives on, giving us songs to cheer us when we are down, inspire us when we are tired, and soothe us when we are troubled.

Breaking into song wherever we are—in the car, in the shower, at work or at play—is second nature to us. The songs we sing are usually the ones we remember from our parents or from our childhood songfests around a campfire.

It is the editors' hope that the songs in this collection will rekindle fond memories of good times, and that these strong memories will become an integral part of keeping our folk song heritage alive.

About the Editors

Irene Maddox has been associated with music in almost every way possible—she has sung, taught music in public schools, been a church accompanist, played professionally in orchestras and Broadway shows; she has performed as a soloist in the United States and Europe in front of symphony orchestras, as part of chamber groups, and as part of a flute-guitar duo. She teaches flute in her Charlotte, North Carolina, studio, as well as on the staff of the University of North Carolina at Charlotte and Queens College. She performs with organist Mark Andersen as the Andersen–Maddox Duo, who record exclusively for International Artists (United States) and Philips (Europe).

A native of Texas and a graduate of North Texas State University, where she received both her BA and MME degrees, Mrs. Maddox has studied in Europe with internationally acclaimed flutist Jean-Pierre Rampal. She is founder of the Charlotte Flute Association and an officer of the National Flute Association. Two daughters, Robirene and Melisande, and husband Robert Maddox, a musician/conductor, make up her family.

Equally at ease singing songs such as those in this book or performing as a soloist before 90,000 people, Mrs. Maddox radiates enthusiasm for music.

Rosalyn Cobb works with both children and adults in many different aspects of music. She has concentrated her efforts in Orff-Music and has developed many programs in this area for children, senior citizens, and handicapped persons. She currently teaches at The Community School of the Arts, which is located in Charlotte, North Carolina.

Ms. Cobb completed her studies in organ and piano at Salem College in Winston-Salem, North Carolina and at The Oberlin Conservatory of Music in Cleveland, Ohio. She has appeared as a piano soloist with The Charlotte Symphony Orchestra and has toured extensively as accompanist of The Charlotte Choirboys.

Teaching summer classes for gifted children in musical theater, directing church choirs, and maintaining a large private studio of piano students have enabled Rosalyn to share with others her enthusiasm for music. Some of her fondest childhood memories are of singing and playing the campfire songs in this book during summer vacations at various camps in the Carolinas.

Get Along Little Dogies
(Whoopee Ti-yi-yo) (Dogie Song)

Cowboy

1. As I was a - walk - ing one morn - ing for pleas - ure, I spied a cow - punch - er a - rid - ing a - long. His hat was thrown back and his spurs were a - jin - gling, And as he ap - proached he was sing - ing this song:

Chorus

Whoo - pee ti - yi - yo,____ get a - long lit- tle do - gies, It's your mis - for- tune and none of my own. Whoo - pee ti - yi -yo,__ get a - long lit - tle do - gies, You know that Wy - o - ming will be your new home.

2. It's early in spring when we round up the dogies,
   And mark them and brand them and bob off their tails,
   We round up our horses and load the chuck wagon,
   And then herd the dogies right out on the trail. *(Chorus)*

Goodbye, Old Paint

Cowboy

1. My foot in the stir-rup, my po-ny won't stan';___ I'm leav-ing Chey-enne and I'm off to Mon-tan'.___

Chorus
Good-bye, old Paint I'm a-leav-ing Chey-enne.

2. I'm riding old Paint and I'm leading old Fan;
   Goodbye little Annie, I'm off for Montan'. *(Chorus)*

3. Oh, keep yourself by me as long as you can;
   Goodbye little Annie, I'm off for Montan'. *(Chorus)*

Home on the Range

Cowboy

1. Oh, give me a home where the buf - fa - lo roam, Where the deer and the an - te - lope play;___ Where sel - dom is heard a dis - cour - a - ging word, And the skies are not cloud - y all day.___

4

Chorus

Home, home on the range,_____ Where the
deer and the an - te - lope play;_____ Where
sel-dom is heard a dis - cour - a- ging word and the
skies are not cloud - y all day._____

2. How often at night when the heavens are bright
   From the light of the glittering stars
   Have I stood there, amazed, and asked as I gazed
   If their glory exceeds that of ours. *(Chorus)*

3. Where the air is so pure and the zephyrs so free,
   And the breezes so balmy and light,
   Oh, I would not exchange my home on the range
   For the glittering cities so bright. *(Chorus)*

4. Oh, give me the land where the bright diamond sand
   Flows leisurely down with the stream,
   Where the graceful, white swan glides slowly along
   Like a maid in a heavenly dream. *(Chorus)*

I Ride an Old Paint

Cowboy

1. I ride an old Paint, ___ I lead an old Dan, ___ I'm goin' to Mon - tan - a to throw the hoo - li - an. They feed in the cou - lees, they wa - ter in the draw, Their tails are all mat - ted, their backs are all raw.

Refrain

Ride a - round lit - tle do - gies, Ride a - round them slow, For they're fier - y and snuf - fy and a rar - in' to go.

2. Oh, when I die, take my saddle from the wall,
   And put it on my pony, lead him out of his stall.
   Tie my bones to his back, turn our faces to the west,
   And we'll ride the prairie that we love the best.

(Refrain)

Red River Valley

Cowboy

1. From this val - ley they say you are

go - ing, ___ We will miss your bright eyes and sweet

smile, For they say you are tak - ing the

sun - shine ___ That bright -ens our path - way a

Refrain

- while. Come and sit by my side if you

love me, ___ Do · not has - ten to bid me a

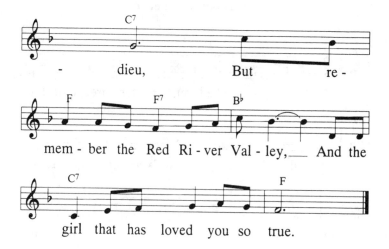

dieu, But re-
mem - ber the Red Ri - ver Val - ley, ___ And the
girl that has loved you so true.

2. Won't you think of the valley you're leaving?
   Oh, how lonely and sad it will be;
   Oh, think of the fond heart you are breaking
   And the grief you are causing to me. *(Refrain)*

3. I have promised you, darling, that never
   Will a word from my lips cause you pain,
   And my life, it shall be yours forever
   If you only will be mine again. *(Refrain)*

4. As you go to your home by the ocean,
   May you never forget those sweet hours
   That we spent in the Red River Valley
   And the love that was ours 'mid the flowers.
                                        (Refrain)

Streets of Laredo
(Cowboy's Lament)

Cowboy

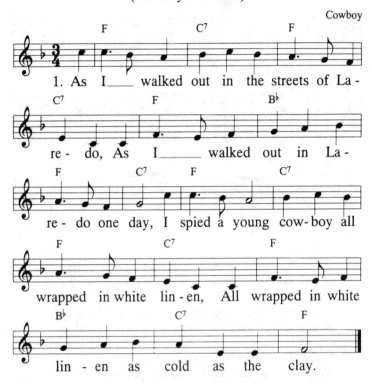

1. As I___ walked out in the streets of La-re-do, As I___ walked out in La-re-do one day, I spied a young cow-boy all wrapped in white lin-en, All wrapped in white lin-en as cold as the clay.

2. "I see by your outfit that you are a cowboy,"
   These words he did say as I boldly stepped by;
   "Come, sit down beside me and hear my sad story,
   I'm shot in the breast and I'm going to die."

3. "Now once in the saddle I used to go dashing,
   Yes, once in the saddle I used to be gay,
   I'd dress myself up and go down to the card-house,
   I got myself shot and I'm dying today."

4. "Get six husky cowboys to carry my coffin,
   Get ten lovely maidens to sing me a song,
   And beat the drum slowly and play the fife lowly,
   For I'm a young cowboy who knows he was wrong."

5. "Oh, please go and bring me a cup of cold water
   To cool my parched lips they are burning," he said,
   Before I could get it, his soul had departed
   And gone to its Maker, the cowboy was dead.

6. We beat the drum slowly and played the fife lowly
   And wept in our grief as we bore him along,
   For we loved the cowboy, so brave and so handsome,
   We loved that young cowboy although he'd done wrong.

Sweet Betsy from Pike

Cowboy

1. Did you ev - er hear of sweet Bet - sy from Pike, Who crossed the wide prai - ries with her hus - band Ike, With two yoke of ox - en, a big yel - low dog, A___ tall Shang - hai roost - er, and one spot - ted hog, Sing - ing *too ra li oo ra li oo ra li ay?*

2. The alkali desert was burning and bare,
   And Ike cried in fear, "We are lost, I declare!
   My dear old Pike Country, I'll come back to you!"
   Vowed Betsy, "You'll go by yourself if you do."
   Singing *too ra li oo ra li oo ra li ay.*

3. 'Twas out on the desert that Betsy gave out,
   And down in the sand she lay rolling about,
   Poor Ike, half distracted, looked down in surprise,
   Saying "Betsy, get up, you'll get sand in your eyes."
   Singing *too ra li oo ra li oo ra li ay.*

4. Then Betsy got up and gazed out on the plain,
   And said she'd go back to Pike Country again,
   But Ike heaved a sigh, and they fondly embraced,
   And they headed on west with his arm 'round her waist.
   Singing *too ra li oo ra li oo ra li ay.*

All My Trials

Spiritual-Lullaby

1. Hush, lit-tle ba-by, don't you cry, You know your Ma-ma was born to die_____ All_____ my tri-als, Lord,_____ soon be o-ver_____ Too late, my bro-thers,_____ Too late but nev-er mind, All_____ my

To Verse 2. Refrain: *

* After 3rd and
  5th verses only.

14

tri - als, Lord,___ soon___ be o - ver.___

2. The river of Jordan is muddy and cold,
   Well, it chills the body, but not the soul,
   (All my trials, Lord, soon be over.)

3. I've got a little book with pages three,
   And ev'ry page spells liberty,
   (All my trials, Lord, soon be over.)

   Too late, my brothers,
   Too late, but never mind,
   (All my trials, Lord, soon be over.)

4. If living were a thing that money could buy,
   You know the rich would live, and the poor would die,
   (All my trials, Lord, soon be over.)

5. There grows a tree in Paradise,
   And the Pilgrims call it the tree of life,
   (All my trials, Lord, soon be over.)

   Too late, my brothers,
   Too late, but never mind,
   (All my trials, Lord, soon be over.)

All Night, All Day

Spiritual

Amazing Grace

Gospel Hymn

1. A - maz - ing___ Grace, how
2. Twas___ grace that___ taught my
3. When___ we've been___ there ten

sweet the sound, That___ saved a___
heart to fear, And___ grace my___
thou - sand years, Bright___ shi - ning___

wretch like___ me.___ I___ once was___
fear re - lieved.___ How___ prec - ious___
as the___ sun,___ We've___ no less___

lost, but___ now I'm found, Was___
did that___ grace ap - pear, The___
days to___ sing God's praise, Than___

blind, but___ now I see.___
hour I___ first be - lieved.___
when we've___ first be - gun.___

(Repeat verse 1)

Down by the Riverside

Spiritual

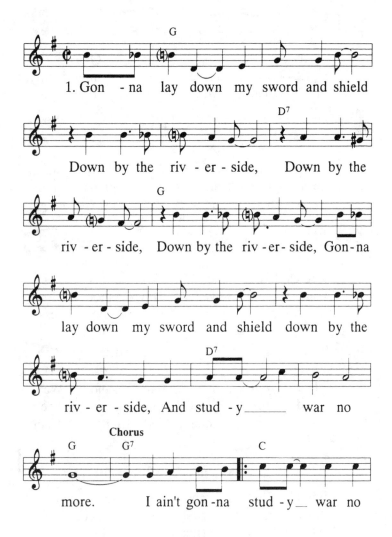

1. Gon - na lay down my sword and shield

Down by the riv - er - side, Down by the

riv - er - side, Down by the riv - er - side, Gon - na

lay down my sword and shield down by the

riv - er - side, And stud - y war no

Chorus

more. I ain't gon -na stud - y war no

18

more, I ain't gon - na stud -y___ war no

more, I ain't gon - na stud -y_____ war no

more___ I ain't gon - na more.___

2. I'm gonna put on my long white robe, etc.
   (Chorus)

3. I'm gonna talk with the Prince of Peace, etc.
   (Chorus)

4. I'm gonna join hands with ev'ryone, etc.
   (Chorus)

Down in my Heart

Spiritual

1. I've got that joy, joy, joy, joy, down in my heart, down in my heart, down in my heart. I've got that joy, joy, joy, joy, down in my heart, down in my heart to-day.

2. I've got that love of Jesus, love of Jesus,
   down in my heart, etc.

3. I've got that peace that passeth understanding
   down in my heart, etc.

Ezekiel Saw the Wheel

Spiritual

E - ze - kiel saw the wheel, 'Way up in the mid - dle of the air; E - ze - kiel saw the wheel, 'Way in the mid - dle of the air; The big wheel runs by faith, Lit - tle wheel runs by the Grace of God, A wheel in a wheel, 'Way in the mid - dle of the

Get on Board

Spiritual

Chorus
Get on board, lit-tle chil-dren, Get on
board, lit-tle chil-dren, Get on board, lit-tle
chil-dren, There's room for man-y a more.

Verse
1. The gos-pel train's a com-ing, I
hear it just at hand, I hear the car wheels
rum-bling, And roll-ing through the land.

2. I hear the train a-coming,
a-coming 'round the curve,
She loosened all her steam and brakes,
she's straining every nerve. *(Chorus)*

3. The fare is cheap and all can go,
the rich and poor are there,
No second class aboard this train,
no difference in the fare. *(Chorus)*

23

Go, Tell It on the Mountain

Spiritual

1. When I was a seek - er, I sought both night and day. I asked the Lord to help me, And He showed me the way.

Chorus Go, tell it on the moun - tain, O - ver the hills and ev - 'ry - where. Go, tell it on the moun - tain, Our

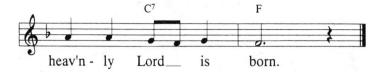

heav'n - ly   Lord ___   is   born.

2. He made me a watchman
   Upon the city wall.
   And if I serve Him truly,
   I am the least of all. *(Chorus)*

3. In the time of David,
   Some said he was a king.
   And if a child is true born,
   The Lord will hear him sing. *(Chorus)*

He's Got the Whole World in His Hands

Spiritual

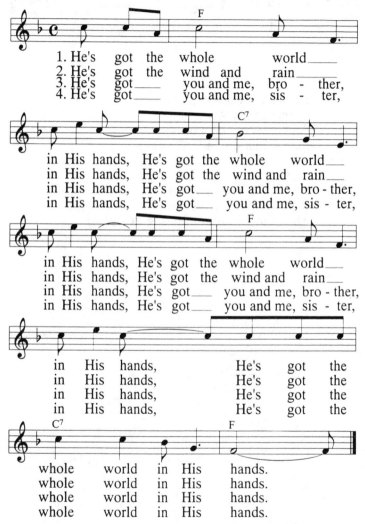

1. He's got the whole world____
2. He's got the wind and rain_____
3. He's got____ you and me, bro - ther,
4. He's got____ you and me, sis - ter,

in His hands, He's got the whole world__
in His hands, He's got the wind and rain__
in His hands, He's got__ you and me, bro - ther,
in His hands, He's got__ you and me, sis - ter,

in His hands, He's got the whole world__
in His hands, He's got the wind and rain__
in His hands, He's got__ you and me, bro - ther,
in His hands, He's got__ you and me, sis - ter,

in His hands, He's got the
in His hands, He's got the
in His hands, He's got the
in His hands, He's got the

whole world in His hands.
whole world in His hands.
whole world in His hands.
whole world in His hands.

I'll Fly Away

Spiritual

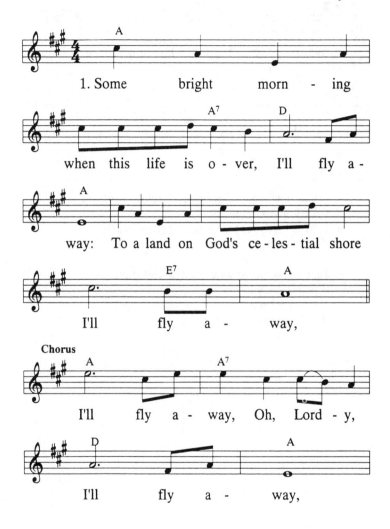

1. Some bright morn - ing when this life is o - ver, I'll fly a - way: To a land on God's ce - les - tial shore I'll fly a - way,

Chorus

I'll fly a - way, Oh, Lord - y, I'll fly a - way,

When I die, hal - le - lu - jah, by and by,

I'll fly a - way.

2. When dark shadows of this life are nigh,
   I'll fly away:
   Like a bird, far from these prison walls
   I'll fly away. *(Chorus)*

3. Just a few more weary days and then,
   I'll fly away:
   To a land where joys will never end
   I'll fly away. *(Chorus)*

I'm On My Way

Chorus:

I'm on my way____ and I won't turn back,____ I'm on my way____ and I won't turn back,____ I'm on my way____ and I won't turn back, I'm on my way, great God, I'm on my way.

Verses:

1. I asked my brother to come with me, etc. *(Chorus)*

2. If he won't come, I'll go along, etc. *(Chorus)*

3. I asked my sister to come with me, etc. *(Chorus)*

4. If she won't come, I'll go alone, etc. *(Chorus)*

5. I'm on my way to Freedom Land, etc. *(Chorus)*

Jacob's Ladder

Spiritual

1. We are— climb - ing— Ja - cobs—
lad - der,— We are— climb - ing—
Ja - cobs— lad - der,— We are—
climb- ing— Ja - cob's— lad - der,—
Sol - diers of the— cross.—

2. Every round goes higher, higher, etc.

3. Brother, do you love my Jesus? etc.

4. If you love Him, you must serve Him, etc.

5. We are climbing higher, higher, etc.

Joshua Fought
the Battle of Jericho

Spiritual

Refrain

Dm

Josh - ua   fought   the   bat - tle   of___

A7   Dm

Jer -i - cho,___   Jer -i - cho,___   Jer -i - cho;___

Dm

Josh - ua   fought   the   bat - tle   of___

A7

Jer - i - cho,___   and the walls   came   tum - bling

Dm   **Verse**   Dm

down.   1. You   may   talk a- bout your   kings of

Gid - e - on,   You   may

31

talk a-bout your men_ of_ Saul, But there's
none like good old Josh - ua at the
bat - tle of Jer - i - cho.

2. Now the Lord commanded Joshua:
   "I command you, and obey you must;
   You just march straight to those city walls
   And the walls will turn to dust." *(Refrain)*

3. Straight up to the walls of Jericho
   He marched with spear in hand,
   "Go blow that ram's horn," Joshua cried,
   "For the battle is in my hand." *(Refrain)*

4. Then the lamb ram sheep horns began to blow,
   And the trumpets began to sound,
   And Joshua commanded, "Now children, shout!"
   And the walls came tumbling down. *(Refrain)*

Keep Your Lamps Trimmed
and Burning

Gospel Hymn

Chorus

Keep your___ lamps trimmed and burn_

___ - ing, Keep your lamps trimmed and burn_

___ - ing, Keep your_ lamps trimmed and burn_

___ - ing,___ the time is draw_ - ing nigh___.

Verses

1. Chil - dren, don't get wear - y, chil - dren,
2. Sis - ter, don't stop pray - in', sis - ter,
3. Bro - ther, don't stop sing - in', broth - er,

don't   get   wear___ - y,   chil - dren,
don't   stop   pray___ -in',   sis - ter,
don't   stop   sing___ -in',   bro - ther,

don't   get   wear - y   'till   your
don't   stop   pray - in' 'till   your
don't   stop   sing - in' 'till   your

work   is___   done.
work   is___   done.
work   is___   done.

34

Lonesome Valley

Spiritual

1. Je - sus walked____ this lone - some val - ley,____ He had to walk__ it by Him - self,____ O no - bod - y else____ could walk it for Him,_____ He had to walk it by____ Him - self.

2. We must walk this lonesome valley,
   we have to walk it by ourselves,
   O nobody else can walk it for us,
   we have to walk it by ourselves.

3. You must go and stand your trial,
   you have to stand it by yourself,
   O nobody else can stand it for you,
   you have to stand it by yourself.

Mary Had a Baby

Spiritual

1. Mar - y had a ba - by, my Lord,
Mar - y had a ba - by, my Lord,
Mar - y had a ba - by, Mar - y had a ba - by,
Mar - y had a ba - by, my Lord.

2. Laid him in a manger, my Lord, etc.

3. She named him King Jesus, my Lord, etc.

4. Shepherds came to see Him, my Lord, etc.

Michael, Row the Boat Ashore

Spiritual

Mich - ael, row the boat a - shore,___ ___ Al - le - lu - ia, Mich - ael, row the boat a - shore,___ Al - le - lu -___ ia.

2. Michael's boat's a music boat, Alleluia,
   Michael's boat's a music boat, Alleluia.

3. Sister, help to trim the sail, Alleluia,
   Sister, help to trim the sail, Alleluia.

4. Jordan's River is deep and wide, Alleluia,
   Kills the body but not the soul, Alleluia.

5. Jordan's River is deep and wide, Alleluia,
   Meet my mother on the other side, Alleluia.

6. Gabriel, blow the trumpet horn, Alleluia,
   Blow the trumpet loud and long, Alleluia.

Nobody Knows the Trouble I've Seen

Spiritual

No-bod-y knows the trou-ble I've seen,

No-bod-y knows but Je - sus.

No-bod-y knows the trou-ble I've seen,

glo - ry hal - le - lu - jah!

1. Some - times I'm up, some -

times I'm down, oh yes,

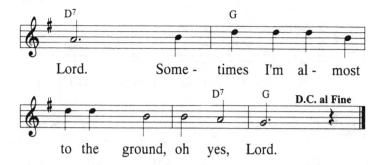

Lord. Some - times I'm al - most to the ground, oh yes, Lord.

2. Although you see me going along slow,
   Oh, yes, Lord,
   I have great trials here below,
   Oh, yes, Lord. *(Refrain)*

3. One day when I was walking along,
   Oh, yes, Lord.
   Heaven opened wide, and love came down,
   Oh, yes, Lord. *(Refrain)*

4. Why does old Satan hate me so?
   Oh, yes, Lord,
   He had me once, then let me go,
   Oh, yes, Lord. *(Refrain)*

5. I never will forget the day,
   Oh, yes, Lord,
   When Jesus washed my sins away,
   Oh, yes, Lord. *(Refrain)*

Oh, Won't You Sit Down?

Spiritual

Chorus

Oh, won't you sit down? Lord, I

can't sit down. Oh, won't you

sit down? Lord, I can't sit down. Oh, won't you

sit down? Lord I can't sit down, 'Cause I

just got to heav - en, goin' to look a - round.

Verse

1. Who's that yon - der dressed in red?
2. Who's that yon - der dressed in blue?

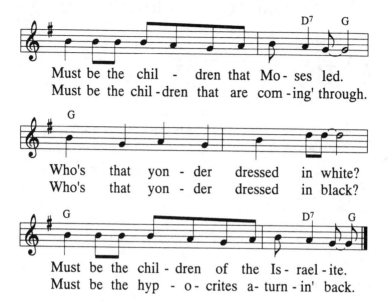

Must be the chil - dren that Mo - ses led.
Must be the chil - dren that are com - ing' through.

Who's that yon - der dressed in white?
Who's that yon - der dressed in black?

Must be the chil - dren of the Is - rael - ite.
Must be the hyp - o - crites a - turn - in' back.

Old Ark's A-Movin'

Spiritual

Chorus:

Old ark's a - mov - in',
mov - in'; chil - dren, won't you
come a - long? Old ark's a -
mov - in': I Re - joice!

Verses:

1. How man - y days did the wa - ter fall?_____
2. See that sis - ter dressed so fine?_ She
3. See those chil - dren dressed in white?_ It
4. See those chil - dren dressed in red?_ It

(Chorus)

For - ty days and nights and all.
ain't got Je - sus on her mind.
must be the chil - dren of the Is - rael - ites.
must be the chil - dren that Mo - ses led.

Old Time Religion

Spiritual

1. Gim - me that old time re - li - gion, Gim - me that old time re - li - gion, Gim - me that old time re - li - gion, It's good e - nough for me.

2. It was good for the Hebrew children, etc.

3. It was good for Paul and Silas, etc.

4. It will take us all to heaven, etc.

One More River

Spiritual

1. Old No-ah built him-self an ark, There's one more riv-er to cross, And built it all of hick-o-ry bark, There's one more riv-er to cross.

Chorus

One more riv-er____ And that's the riv-er of Jor - dan;

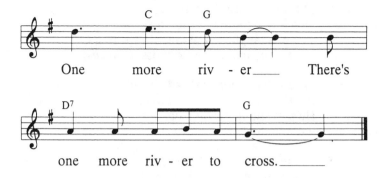

One more riv - er____ There's one more riv - er to cross.____

2. The animals came two by two,
   there's one more river to cross,
   The elephant and kangaroo,
   there's one more river to cross. *(Chorus)*

3. The animals came three by three,
   there's one more river to cross,
   The baboon and the chimpanzee,
   there's one more river to cross. *(Chorus)*

4. The animals came four by four,
   there's one more river to cross,
   Old Noah got mad and hollered for more,
   there's one more river to cross. *(Chorus)*

5. The animals came five by five,
   there's one more river to cross,
   The bees came swarming from the hive,
   there's one more river to cross. *(Chorus)*

6. The animals came six by six,
   there's one more river to cross,
   The lion laughed at the monkey's tricks,
   there's one more river to cross. *(Chorus)*

7. When Noah found he had no sail,
   there's one more river to cross,
   He just ran up his old coat tail,
   there's one more river to cross. *(Chorus)*

8. Before the voyage did begin,
   there's one more river to cross,
   Old Noah pulled the gangplank in,
   there's one more river to cross. *(Chorus)*

9. They never knew where they were at,
   there's one more river to cross,
   'Til the old ark bumped on Ararat,
   there's one more river to cross. *(Chorus)*

Rise and Shine

Spiritual

Rise___ and shine___, and give God the
glo - ry, glo - ry, Rise___ and shine___, and
give God the glo - ry, glo - ry, Rise and
shine and give God the glo - ry, glo - ry,
chil - dren of the Lord.___

1. The Lord said to No-ah, "There's gon -na be a

flood -y flood - y" (The) Lord said to No - ah, "There's gon - na be a flood - y flood - y. Get your chil - dren out of the mud - dy, mud - dy!" Chil -dren of the Lord.

2. So No-ah, he built him, he built him an ark-y ark-y;
   So No-ah, he built him, he built him an ark-y ark-y;
   Built it out of hick'ry bark-y bark-y,
   Children of the Lord. *(Chorus)*

3. The animals, they came, they came by two-sies, two-sies;
   The animals, they came, they came by two-sies, two-sies;
   Elephants and kang-a-roo-sies, roo-sies,
   Children of the Lord. *(Chorus)*

4. It rained and poured for forty day-sies, day-sies;
   (It) rained and poured for forty day-sies, day-sies;
   Drove those animals nearly crazy, crazy,
   Children of the Lord. *(Chorus)*

5. The sun came out and dried up the land-y, land-y;
   The sun came out and dried up the land-y, land-y;
   Ev-'ry-one felt fine and dandy, dandy,
   Children of the Lord. *(Chorus)*

Rock-a-My-Soul

Spiritual

Rock - a - my soul in the bo - som of A - bra - ham;

Rock - a - my soul in the bo - som of A - bra - ham;

Rock - a - my soul in the bo - som of A - bra - ham

Oh, rock - a my soul. 1. My Lord is
2. His love is

so high, you can't get o - ver Him;
so high, you can't get o - ver it;

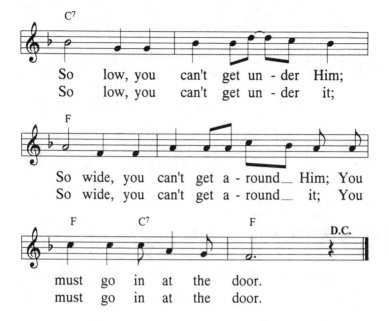

So   low, you   can't   get un - der   Him;
So   low, you   can't   get un - der   it;

So   wide, you   can't   get a - round_ Him; You
So   wide, you   can't   get a - round_ it; You

must   go   in   at   the   door.
must   go   in   at   the   door.

Somebody's Knockin' at Your Door

Spiritual

knock - in' at your door. Knocks like__ Je - sus, *Some -bod -y's knock - in' at your* door. O_____ sin - ner, why don't you an - swer? *Some - bod - y's knock -in' at your door. Hal - le - lu.*

Standin' In the Need of Prayer

Spiritual

It's me, it's me, O Lord,

stand - in' in the need of prayer. It's

me, it's me, O Lord,

stand - in' in the need of prayer.

Verse

1. Not my broth - er, not my sis - ter, but it's

me, O Lord, Stand - in' in the need of

prayer; Not my broth - er, not my sis - ter, but it's me, O Lord, stand - in' in the need of prayer.

2. Not my father, not my mother,
   but it's me, O Lord,
   Standin' in the need of prayer, etc. *(Chorus)*

3. Not my preacher, not my teacher,
   but it's me, O Lord,
   Standin' in the need of prayer, etc. *(Chorus)*

Steal Away

Spiritual

Steal a-way, steal a-way,

steal a-way to Je-sus.

Steal a-way, steal a-way home, I

don't have long to stay here.

Verse

1. My Lord___ calls me, He
2. Green trees are bend-ing, poor
3. My Lord he calls me, He

56

calls me by the thun - der; The
sin - ners they stand tremb - ling, The
calls me by the light - ning, The

trum - pet sounds with - in __ my soul, I
trum - pet sounds with - in __ my soul, I
trum - pet sounds with - in __ my soul, I

don't have long to stay here.
don't have long to stay here.
don't have long to stay here.

There's a Little Wheel A-Turning

Spiritual

1. There's a lit-tle wheel a-turn-ing in my heart, There's a lit-tle wheel a-turn-ing in my heart. In my heart, in my heart, There's a lit-tle wheel a-turn-ing in my heart.

2. Oh, I feel so very happy in my heart,
   Oh, I feel so very happy in my heart.
   In my heart, in my heart,
   Oh, I feel so very happy in my heart.

This Train

Spiritual

1. This train is bound for glo - ry, This train,__

This train is bound for glo - ry, This train,__

This train is bound for glo - ry

Don't ride noth - in' but the good and ho - ly,

This train is bound for glo-ry, This train!

2. This train don't pull no extras, This train,
   This train don't pull no extras, This train,
   This train don't pull no extras,
   Don't pull nothin' but the midnight special,
   This train don't pull no extras, This train!

Wade in the Water

Leader Sings
All Sing

Spiritual

Chorus

Wade____ in the wa - ter,____

Wade in the wa - ter, chil - dren, Wade in the

wa - ter,____ God's goin' to trou - ble the

wa - ter____ *(Leader)* 1. See that band all

(Leader) 2. See that band all

dressed in white!__ *God's goin' to trou - ble the*

dressed in red!___ *God's goin' to trou - ble the*

wa - ter.__ The lead - er____ looks like the
wa - ter.__ It must be the band that____

Is - rael - ite. *God's goin' to trou - ble the*
Mos - es led. *God's goin' to trou - ble the*

(Chorus)

wa - ter.____
wa - ter.____

Wayfaring Stranger

Spiritual

1. I'm just a poor way - far - ing strang - er, A trav -'ling through this world of woe; But there's no sick - ness, toil nor dan - ger in that bright world to which I go. I'm go - ing there to see my fa - ther,* I'm go - ing there no more to

roam; I'm just a - go - ing o - ver

Jor - dan, I'm just a - go - ing o - ver home.

* 2. mother   3. sister   4. brother

When the Saints Go Marching In

Spiritual

1. Oh, when the Saints__ go march-ing in,__ Oh, when the Saints go march-ing in,__ Oh, Lord, I want to be in that num-ber__ When the Saints go march-ing in.__

2. And when the revelation comes,
   And when the revelation comes,
   Oh, Lord, I want to be in that number,
   When the revelation comes.

Continue, as above:

3. Oh, when the new world is revealed...
4. Oh, when they gather 'round the throne...
5. And when they crown Him King of Kings...
6. And when the sun no more will shine...
7. And when the moon has turned to blood...
8. And when the earth has turned to fire...
9. And on that hallelujah day...
10. Oh, when the Saints go marching in...

The Barnyard Song

Kentucky Mountains
Folk Song

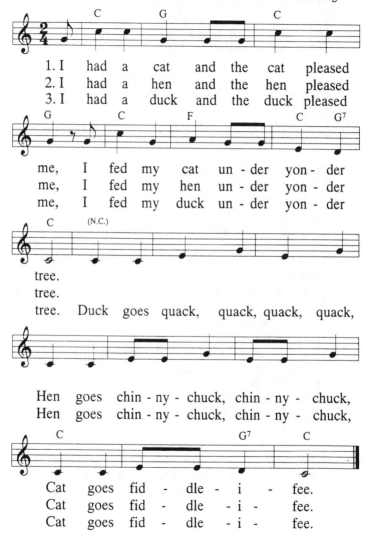

1. I had a cat and the cat pleased
2. I had a hen and the hen pleased
3. I had a duck and the duck pleased

me, I fed my cat un - der yon - der
me, I fed my hen un - der yon - der
me, I fed my duck un - der yon - der

tree.
tree.
tree. Duck goes quack, quack, quack, quack,

Hen goes chin - ny - chuck, chin - ny - chuck,
Hen goes chin - ny - chuck, chin - ny - chuck,

Cat goes fid - dle - i - fee.
Cat goes fid - dle - i - fee.
Cat goes fid - dle - i - fee.

4. I had a goose and the goose pleased me,
   I fed my goose under yonder tree.
   Goose goes swishy, swashy,
   Duck goes quack, quack, quack, quack,
   Cat goes fiddle-i-fee.

5. I had a sheep and the sheep pleased me,
   I fed my sheep under yonder tree.
   Sheep goes baa, baa,
   Goose goes swishy, swashy,
   Cat goes fiddle-i-fee.

6. I had a pig and the pig pleased me,
   I fed my pig under yonder tree.
   Pig goes griffy, gruffy,
   Sheep goes baa, baa,
   Cat goes fiddle-i-fee.

7. I had a cow and the cow pleased me.
   I fed my cow under yonder tree.
   Cow goes moo, moo,
   Pig goes griffy, gruffy,
   Cat goes fiddle-i-fee.

8. I had a horse and the horse pleased me.
   I fed my horse under yonder tree.
   Horse goes neigh, neigh,
   Cow goes moo, moo,
   Cat goes fiddle-i-fee.

With each stanza repeat what the different animals say in the preceding stanza, always ending with "Cat goes fiddle-i-fee."

Bicycle Built For Two
(Daisy Bell)

Harry Dacre
American Folk

Dai - sy, Dai - sy, give me your an - swer true, I'm half cra - zy all for the love of you.___ It won't be a styl - ish mar - riage; I can't af - ford a car - riage,___ But you'll look sweet on the seat of a bi - cy - cle built for two.___

The Blue Tail Fly
(Jimmy Crack Corn)

Dan Emmett

American Folk

When I was young I used to wait on

mas - ter and give him his plate, and

pass the bot - tle when he got dry, And

brush a - way the blue tail fly.

Jim - my crack corn and I don't care,

Jim - my crack corn and I don't care,

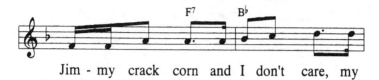

Jim - my crack corn and I don't care, my

mas - ter's gone a - way.

Bound for the Promised Land

Early American Folk Song

1. On___ Jor - dan's storm___ - y banks I stand and cast a wish__ - ful eye, To___ Ca - naan's fair and hap - py land where my pos - ses - sions
2. Oh___ the trans - port___ - ing rapt' - rous scene that ri - ses to___ my sight. Sweet__ fields ar__ rayed in liv - ing green, and__ riv - ers__ of de -
3. There___ gen - 'rous fruits__ that nev - er fail on trees im - mor__ - tal grow; There__ rocks and__ hills and brooks and vales with__ milk and__ ho - ney
4. Soon___ will the Lord__ my soul pre - pare for joys be - yond__ the skies; Where__ nev - er__ ceas - ing pleas - ures roll, and__ prais - es__ nev - er

lie.
light.
flow.
die.

I am bound for the prom - ised

land,_____ I'm bound for the prom - ised

land; O_____ who will__come and

go with me? I am bound for the prom - ised

land.

Buffalo Gals

American Folk Song

1. As I was wan - d'ring down the street, down the street, down the street, a pret - ty girl I chanced to meet, oh, she was fair to view.

Refrain

Then Buf - fa - lo gals, will you come out to - night, will you

come out to - night, will you
come out to - night, Then Buf-fa-lo gals, will you
come out to - night, And
dance by the light of the moon?

2. I stopped her and I had some talk,
   had some talk, had some talk,
   Her foot covered up the whole sidewalk,
   and left no room for me. *(Refrain)*

3. She's the prettiest gal I've seen in my life,
   seen in my life, seen in my life,
   I wish that she could be my wife,
   Then we would part no more. *(Refrain)*

Cindy

Appalachia

1. I wish I had a nick - el, I wish I had a

dime, I wish I had a pret -ty girl to love me all the

time. Get a- long home, Cin - dy,

Cin - dy, Get a- long home, Cin - dy,

Cin - dy, Get a- long home, Cin - dy,

Cin - dy, I'll mar - ry you some day.

2. You ought to see my Cindy,
   She lives a-way down south,
   And she's so sweet the honey bees,
   Swarm around her mouth. *(Chorus)*

3. The first time I saw Cindy,
   She was standing in the door.
   Her shoes and stockings in her hand,
   Her feet all over the floor. *(Chorus)*

4. She took me to the parlor,
   She cooled me with her fan,
   She said I was the prettiest thing,
   In the shape of mortal man. *(Chorus)*

5. I wish I were an apple,
   A-hanging on a tree,
   And every time my Cindy passed,
   She'd take a bite of me. *(Chorus)*

6. I wish I had a needle,
   As fine as I could sew,
   I'd sew that gal to my coat tail,
   And down the road I'd go. *(Chorus)*

Clementine

U.S.

1. In a cav - ern, in a can - yon, Ex - ca-

vat - ing for a mine, Dwelt a

min - er for - ty - nin - er, And his

daugh - ter Clem - en - tine.

Chorus

Oh, my dar - ling, Oh, my

dar - ling, Oh, my dar - ling Clem - en -

tine! You are lost and gone for -
ev - er, Dread -ful sor - ry, Clem - en - tine!

2. Light she was, and like a fairy,
   And her shoes were number nine,
   Herring boxes without topses,
   Sandals were for Clementine. *(Chorus)*

3. Drove she ducklings to the water
   Every morning just at nine,
   Hit her foot against a splinter,
   fell into the foaming brine. *(Chorus)*

4. Ruby lips above the water
   Blowing bubbles soft and fine;
   As for me, I was no swimmer
   And I lost my Clementine. *(Chorus)*

5. How I missed her, how I missed her,
   How I missed my Clementine.
   Then I kissed her little sister,
   And forgot dear Clementine. *(Chorus)*

Down by the Old Millstream

American Folk Song

Down by the old mill -

stream, Where I first met

you, With your eyes so

blue, dressed in ging - ham,

too. It was there I

knew, That you loved me

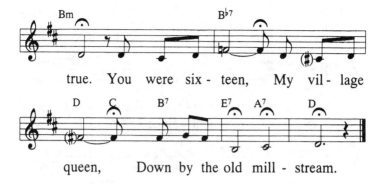

true. You were six - teen, My vil - lage

queen, Down by the old mill - stream.

The version of this song that appears below adds opposites to some
words in each line. The additional words are sung on the same note
as the immediately preceding word--except the final phrase, which is
sung very, very slowly to the tune of the equivalent phrase of "How
Dry I Am".

Down by the old (not the new, but the old)
   millstream (not the river, but the stream),
Where I first (not last, but first)
   met you (not me, but you),
With your eyes (not your ears, but your eyes)
   so blue (not green, but blue),
Dressed in gingham (not silk, but gingham)
   too (not one, but two).
It was there (not here, but there)
   I knew (not old, but knew),
That I loved (not hated, but loved)
   you true (not false, but true).
You were sixteen (not fifteen, but sixteen),
My village queen (not the king, but the queen),
Down by the old (not the new, but the old)
   millstream (not the river, but the stream).

Down in the Valley

Kentucky

1. Down in the val - ley the val - ley so
2. Ros - es love sun - shine, vio - lets love

low, Hang your head o - ver, hear the winds
dew, An - gels in hea - ven know I love

blow. Hear the winds blow, dear, hear the winds
you. Know I love you, dear, know I

blow, Hang your head o -ver, hear the winds blow.
you, An - gels in hea-ven know I love you.

Erie Canal

U.S.

I've got a mule, her name is Sal, Fif-teen miles on the E-rie Ca-nal. She's a good old work-er and a good old pal, Fif-teen miles on the E-rie Ca-nal. We've hauled some barg-es in our day, Filled with lumb-er, coal and hay, And we know eve-ry inch of the way from

Al - ba - ny to___ Buf___ - fa - lo.___

Chorus

Low   bridge,   eve - ry - bod - y   down,

Low   bridge,   'cause   we're

com - ing   to a   town;   And   you'll

al - ways   know   your   neigh - bor,   You'll

al - ways   know   your   pal,   if   you've

ev - er   nav - i - gat - ed   on   the

E - rie   Ca - nal.

The Glendy Burk

Stephen C. Foster

1. The *Glen - dy Burk* is a might-y fast boat, With a might-y fast cap-tain, too; He sits up there on the hur - ri - cane roof, And he keeps an eye on the crew.

I can't stay here for the work too hard, I'm bound to leave this town; I'll take my duds and tote 'em on my back, When the

Glen - dy Burk comes down.

Chorus

Ho! for Lou' - si - an - a! I'm

bound to leave this town, I'll

take my duds and tote 'em on my back, When the

Glen - dy Burk comes down.

2. The *Glendy Burk* has a funny old crew,
and they sing the boatman's song,
They burn the pitch and the pine knot, too,
just to shove the boat along;
The smoke goes up and the engine roars
and the wheel goes round and round,
Then fare you well, for I'll take a little ride
when the *Glendy Burk* comes down.

Good Night, Ladies

U.S.

1. Good night, la-dies,__ Good night, la-dies__ Good night, la-dies,__ We're going to leave you now._____ Mer-ri-ly we roll a-long, roll a-long, roll a-long, Mer-ri-ly we roll a-long, O'er the dark blue sea.

Hush, Little Baby

U.S.

1. Hush, lit - tle ba - by, don't say a word,

Dad - dy's gon - na buy you a mock - ing bird, And

if that mock - ing bird won't sing,

Dad - dy's gon - na buy you a dia - mond ring. (And)

2. And if that diamond ring turns to brass,
   Daddy's gonna buy you a looking glass,
   And if that looking glass gets broke,
   Daddy's gonna buy you a billy goat.

3. And if that billy goat won't pull,
   Daddy's gonna buy you a cart and bull,
   And if that cart and bull turn over,
   Daddy's gonna buy you a dog named Rover.

4. And if that dog named Rover won't bark,
   Daddy's gonna buy you a horse and cart,
   And if that horse and cart fall down,
   You'll still be the sweetest little baby in town.

I've Been Working on the Railroad
(Dinah)

U.S.

I've been work - ing on the rail - road

all the live -long day; I've been work-ing on the

rail - road to pass the time a - way.

Don't you hear the whis - tle blow - ing?

Rise up so ear - ly in the morn.

Don't you hear the cap - tain shout - ing,

"Di - nah, blow your horn!"

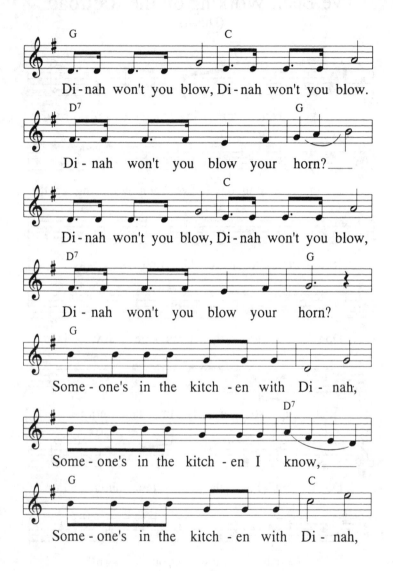

Di-nah won't you blow, Di-nah won't you blow.

Di - nah won't you blow your horn?___

Di-nah won't you blow, Di-nah won't you blow,

Di - nah won't you blow your horn?

Some - one's in the kitch - en with Di - nah,

Some - one's in the kitch - en I know,___

Some - one's in the kitch - en with Di - nah,

Strum - ming on the old ban - jo.

Fee fie fid - dle - ee - i - o,

Fee fie fid - dle - ee - i - o,____

Fee fie fid - dle - ee - i - o,

Strum - ming on the old ban - jo.

Little 'Liza Jane

U.S.

You got a gal and I got none,

Lit - tle 'Li - za Jane; Come my love and

be my one, Lit - tle 'Li - za Jane.

Chorus

Oh, E - li - za, Lit - tle 'Li - za Jane;

Oh, E - li - za, Lit - tle 'Li - za Jane.

Looby Loo

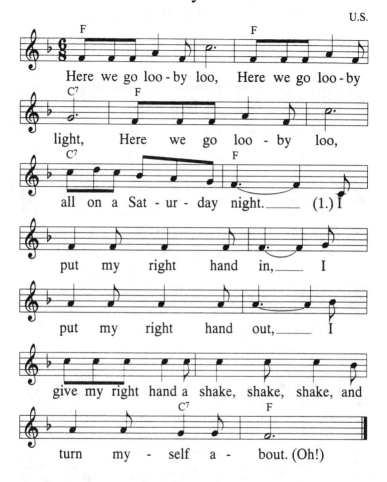

Here we go loo - by loo, Here we go loo - by
light, Here we go loo - by loo,
all on a Sat - ur - day night.＿＿ (1.) I
put my right hand in,＿＿ I
put my right hand out,＿＿ I
give my right hand a shake, shake, shake, and
turn my - self a - bout. (Oh!)

2. I put my left hand in, etc.
3. I put my right foot in, etc.
4. I put my left foot in, etc.
5. I put my head right in, etc.
6. I put my whole self in, etc.

91

The Man Who Has Plenty of Good Peanuts

American Folk Song

The man who has plen - ty of
He shan't__ have an - y of

good pea- nuts, and giv -eth his neigh- bor none,
my pea-nuts, when his__ pea -nuts are gone.

When his pea - nuts are gone.__

When his pean - nuts are gone____ He

shan't have an - y of my pea - nuts when

his pea - nuts are gone!___ Oh, that will be

joy - ful, joy - ful, joy - ful!

Oh, that will be joy - ful, when

his pea - nuts are gone!___

Mountain Dew

American Folk Song

1. Down the road here from me there's an old hol - low tree, Where you lay down a dol - lar or two, If you hush up your mug they will fill up your jug with that good old___ moun - tain dew. They call it that

good old moun-tain dew, And
them that re-fuse it are few.
You may go 'round the
bend, but you'll come back a-gain for that
good old___ moun-tain___ dew.

2. My uncle Bill has a still on the hill,
Where he runs off a gallon or two.
You can tell if you sniff and you get a good whiff
That he's making that good old mountain dew. *(Chorus)*

3. The preacher came by with a tear in his eye,
   He said that his wife had the flu.
   We told him he ought to give her a quart
   Of that good old mountain dew. *(Chorus)*

4. My brother Mort is sawed off and short,
   He measures just four-foot-two;
   But he thinks he's a giant when they give him a pint
   Of that good old mountain dew. *(Chorus)*

My Bonnie

U.S.

1. My Bon - nie lies o - ver the o - cean,
2. Oh, blow ye winds o - ver the o - cean,

My Bon - nie lies o - ver the sea,
Oh, blow ye winds o - ver the sea,

My Bon - nie lies o - ver the o - cean,
Oh, blow ye winds o - ver the o - cean,

Oh, bring back my Bon - nie to me.
And bring back my Bon - nie to me.

Bring back, bring back, Bring back my

Bon - nie to me, to me. me.

97

Oh, Susanna

Stephen Foster

1. I____ came from Al - a -
2. It____ rained all night the

ba - ma With my ban - jo on my
day I left, The weath -er it was

knee. I'm____ going to Loui - si -
dry; The____ sun so hot I

an - a My____ true love for to
froze to death; Su - san - na, don't you

see;
cry.

Oh, Su - san - na, Oh,

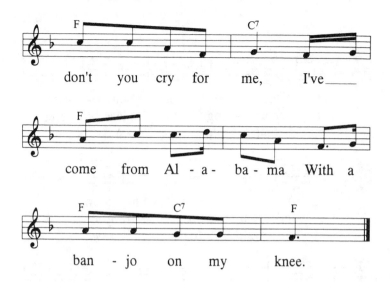

don't you cry for me, I've_____

come from Al - a - ba - ma With a

ban - jo on my knee.

On Top of Old Smokey

U.S.

1. On top of old Smo — key___
2. Oh, court - ing is plea - sure___
3. A thief will just rob you___

___ All cov - ered with snow,___
___ and part - ing is grief,___
___ of all that you save,___

I lost my true lov - er___
But a false heart - ed lov - er___
But a false heart - ed lov - er___

___ By___ court - ing too
___ is___ worse than a
___ will___ lead to the

slow.___
thief.___
grave.___

Over the River
And Through the Wood

Lydia Maria Childs

U.S.

O - ver the riv - er and through the wood, To

grand - fa - ther's house we go:____ The

horse knows the way to

car - ry the sleigh, Through the

white and drift - ed snow.____

O - ver the riv - er and through the wood, Oh,

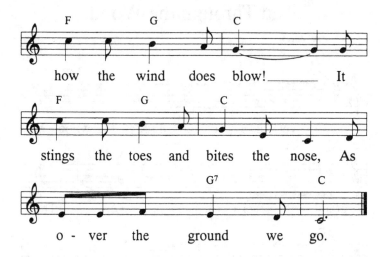

how the wind does blow!_____ It

stings the toes and bites the nose, As

o - ver the ground we go.

Polly Wolly Doodle

American Folk Song

1. Oh, I went down South for to see my Sal, Sing - ing
Pol - ly Wol - ly Doo - dle all the day; My Sal, she is a spunk - y gal, Sing - ing
Pol - ly Wol - ly Doo - dle all the

2. Oh, my Sal she is a maid - en fair, Sing - ing
Pol - ly Wol - ly Doo - dle all the day; With curl - y eyes and laugh - ing hair, Sing - ing
Pol - ly Wol - ly Doo - dle all the

day. Fare thee well, fare thee well, Fare thee
day.

103

well my fair - ry fay, For I'm

goin' to Loui - si - an - a, For to

see my Su - sy - an - a, Sing - ing

Pol - ly Wol - ly Doo - dle all the day.

Reuben and Rachel

U.S.

(Girls) 1. Reu - ben, Reu - ben, I've been think - ing
(Boys) O my good - ness' gra - cious, Ra - chel,

what a grand world this would be,
what a strange world this would be,

If the men were all trans - port - ed
If the men were all trans - port - ed

far be - yond the North - ern Sea.
far be - yond the North - ern Sea.

2. *(girls)*   Reuben, Reuben, I've been thinking
What a fine life girls would lead
If they had no men about them,
None to tease them, none to heed.

(boys)   Rachel, Rachel, I've been thinking
Men would have a merry time
If at once they were transported
Far beyond the salty brine.

The Riddle Song

Kentucky

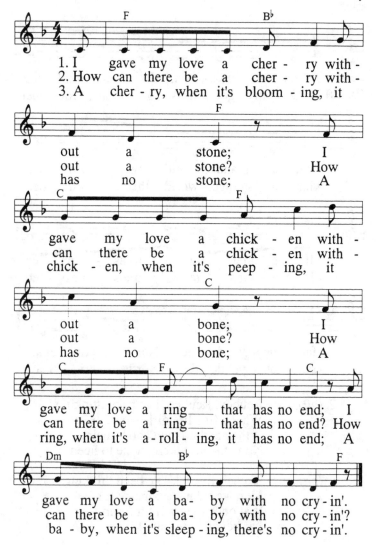

1. I gave my love a cher - ry with -
2. How can there be a cher - ry with -
3. A cher - ry, when it's bloom - ing, it

out a stone; I
out a stone? How
has no stone; A

gave my love a chick - en with -
can there be a chick - en with -
chick - en, when it's peep - ing, it

out a bone; I
out a bone? How
has no bone; A

gave my love a ring___ that has no end; I
can there be a ring___ that has no end? How
ring, when it's a - roll - ing, it has no end; A

gave my love a ba - by with no cry - in'.
can there be a ba - by with no cry - in'?
ba - by, when it's sleep - ing, there's no cry - in'.

She'll Be Comin' 'Round the Mountain

American Folk

1. She'll be com - in' 'round the moun - tain when she comes, ___ She'll be com - in' 'round the moun - tain when she comes, ___ She'll be com - in' 'round the

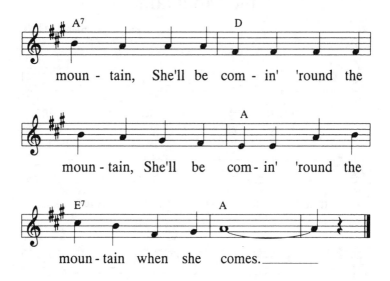

moun - tain, She'll be com - in' 'round the

moun - tain, She'll be com - in' 'round the

moun - tain when she comes._____

2. She'll be drivin' six white horses when she comes,...

3. Oh, we'll all go out to meet her when she comes,...

4. Oh, we'll kill the old red rooster when she comes,...

5. And we'll all have chicken dumplings when she comes,

Shoo, Fly

U.S.

Shoo, fly, don't both - er me, Shoo, fly, don't

both - er me, Shoo, fly, don't both - er me, For

I be - long to some - bod - y. I

feel, I feel, I feel, I feel like a morn - ing

star, I feel, I feel, I feel, I

feel, like a morn - ing star. So, Shoo, fly, don't

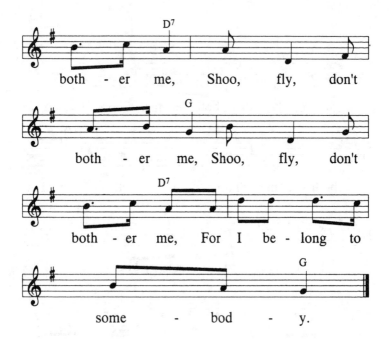

both - er me, Shoo, fly, don't

both - er me, Shoo, fly, don't

both - er me, For I be - long to

some - bod - y.

Skip to My Lou

American Folk Song

Flies in the but - ter - milk, Shoo fly, shoo,

Flies in the but - ter - milk, Shoo fly, shoo,

Flies in the but - ter - milk, Shoo fly, shoo,

Skip to my lou, my dar - ling.

Chorus

Lou, lou, Skip to my lou,

Lou, lou, Skip to my lou,

Lou, lou, Skip to my lou,

Skip to my lou, my dar - ling.

Sourwood Mountain

American Folk

1. Chick-en crow-ing on Sour-wood Moun-tain

Hey de ing dang did - dle al - ly day.

So man-y pret-ty girls I can't count them,

Hey de ing dang did - dle al - ly day.

My true love, she lives in Letch - er,

Hey de ing dang did - dle al - ly day.

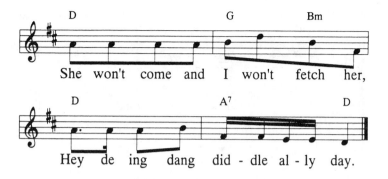

She won't come and I won't fetch her,
Hey de ing dang did - dle al - ly day.

2. My true love's a blue-eyed daisy, Hey, etc.
   If I don't get her I'll go crazy, Hey, etc.
   Big dogs bark and little ones bite you, Hey, etc.
   Big girls court and little ones slight you, Hey, etc.

3. My true love lives by the river, Hey, etc.
   A few more jumps and I'll be with her, Hey, etc.
   My true love lives up the hollow, Hey, etc.
   She won't come and I won't follow, Hey, etc.

Tell Me Why

American Folk Song

1. Tell_____ me why_____ the
2. Be - cause God made_____ the

stars do shine, Tell_____ me
stars to shine, Be - cause God

why_____ the i - vy twines,
made_____ the i - vy twine,

Tell_____ me why_____ the
Be - cause God made_____ the

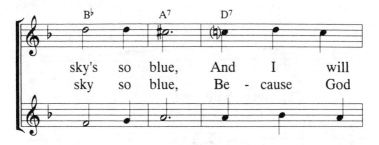

sky's so blue, And I will
sky so blue, Be - cause God

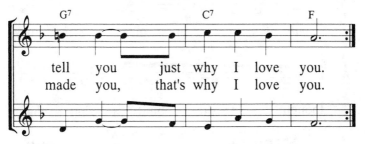

tell you just why I love you.
made you, that's why I love you.

The Titanic

American Folk Song

1. Oh, they built the ship *Ti - tan - ic,* to
sail the o - cean blue; And they
thought they'd built a ship that
wa - ter would not go through; But the
Lord's al - might - y hand said that
ship could nev - er stand: It was

sad___ when that great___ ship went down. It was sad, it was sad, It was sad when that great___ ship went down. Hus - bands and wives, lit - tle chil - dren lost their lives, it was sad__ when the great__ ship went down.

2. Oh, they sailed from England's shore
   'bout a thousand miles or more;
   And the rich folk,
   they re-fused to 'sociate with the poor;
   So, they put them down below,
   where they'd be the first to go,
   It was sad when the great ship went down. *(Chorus)*

3. Oh, the boat was full of sin, and the sides about to burst,
   When the captain yelled for all the women to go first,
   Oh, the captain tried to wire, but the lines were all on fire
   It was sad when that great ship went down. *(Chorus)*

4. Oh, they swung the lifeboats out on the deep and raging sea,
   And the entire band struck up with "Nearer My God to Thee."
   All the children wept and cried,
   As the waves swept o'er the side,
   It was sad when the great ship went down. *(Chorus)*

The Water Is Wide

Early American Folk Song

1. The wa - ter is wide, ____ I can - not get
o - ver. And nei - ther
have ____ I wings to __ fly ____. Give me a
boat ____ that can car - ry two, ____ and both shall
cross, ____ my true love and I ____.

2. I leaned my back against an oak,
   Thinking it was a mighty tree,
   But first it bent and then it broke,
   So did my love prove false to me.

3. I put my hand in some soft bush,
   Thinking the sweetest flower to find,
   I pricked my finger to the bone,
   And left the sweetest flower behind.

4. Oh, love is handsome; love is fine,
   Gay as a jewel when it is new,
   But love grows old and waxes cold,
   And fades away like morning dew.

5. (Repeat verse 1.)

Yankee Doodle

U.S.

1. O fath'r and I went

down to camp, a- long with Cap - tain

Good' - in, And there we saw the

men and boys as thick as hast - y

pud - din'. **Chorus** Yan - kee Doo - dle

keep it up, Yan - kee Doo - dle Dan — - dy,

Mind the mu - sic and the step, And
with the girls be hand - y.

2. And there we saw a thousand men
    As rich as Squire David;
    And what they wasted ev'ry day,
    I wish it could be saved. *(Chorus)*

3. And there was Captain Washington
    Upon a slapping stallion,
    A-giving orders to his men;
    I guess there was a million. *(Chorus)*

4. And then the feathers on his head,
    They looked so very fine, ah!
    I wanted peskily to get
    To give to my Jemima. *(Chorus)*

5. And there I saw a swamping gun,
    Large as a log of maple,
    Upon a mighty little cart;
    A load for father's cattle. *(Chorus)*

Are You Sleeping?

(Frere Jacques) Brother John)

Round

1. Are you sleep - ing, are you sleep - ing,
   Fre - re Jac - ques, Fre - re Jac - ques,

2. Broth - er John, Broth - er John?
   dor - mez - vous, dor - mez - vous?

3. Morn - ing bells are ring - ing,
   Son - nez les ma - ti - nes,

   morn - ing bells are ring - ing,
   Son - nez les ma - ti - nes,

4. Ding, ding, dong,
   din, dan, don,

   ding, ding, dong.
   din, dan, don.

Dona Nobis Pacem

3-part Round (Latin)

124

Hey, Ho! Anybody Home?

Traditional Round

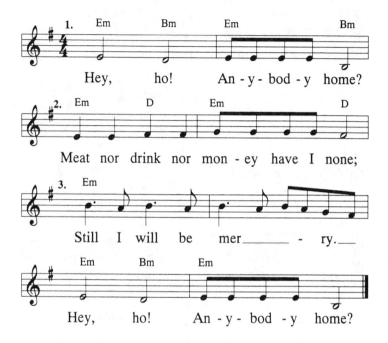

Hey, ho! An - y - bod - y home?

Meat nor drink nor mon - ey have I none;

Still I will be mer——— - ry.——

Hey, ho! An - y - bod - y home?

I Love the Mountains

5-part Round

I love the moun - tains, I love the rol - ling hills,

I love the flow - ers, I love the daf - fo - dils,

I love the fire_-side When all the lights are low,

Boom - dee - ah - da, boom - dee - ah - da,

Boom - dee - ah - da, boom - dee - ah - da,

Boom - dee - ah - da, boom - dee - ah - da,

Boom - dee - ah - da, boom - de - ah - da,

Kookaburra

M. Sinclair

Round from Australia

Kook-a-bur-ra sits on an old gum tree,___

Mer-ry, mer-ry king of the bush is he.___

Laugh, kook-a-bur-ra, laugh, kook-a-bur-ra

Gay your life must be.

Lovely Evening

Three-part Round

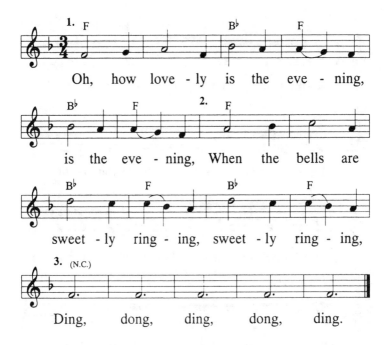

Oh, how love - ly is the eve - ning, is the eve - ning, When the bells are sweet - ly ring - ing, sweet - ly ring - ing, Ding, dong, ding, dong, ding.

Rise Up, O Flame

2-part Round (Praetorious)

Rose, Rose

4-part Round

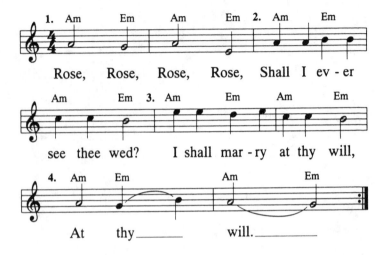

Rose, Rose, Rose, Rose, Shall I ev - er

see thee wed? I shall mar - ry at thy will,

At thy_____ will._____

Row, Row, Row Your Boat

Round

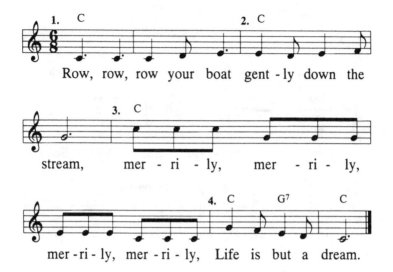

Row, row, row your boat gent - ly down the stream, mer - ri - ly, mer - ri - ly, mer - ri - ly, mer - ri - ly, Life is but a dream.

Shalom Chaverim

8-part Israeli Round

Sha - lom Cha - ve - rim Sha -
lom Cha - ve - rim Sha - lom Sha -
lom L' hit ra____ - ot L'
hit ra____ - ot, sha - lom Sha____ - lom.

White Coral Bells

Round from England

1. White cor - al bells up -
2. Oh, don't you wish that

on a slen - der stalk,
you could hear them ring?

Lil - ies of the val - ley deck my
That will hap - pen on - ly when the

gar - den walk.
fair - ies sing.

133

Blow the Man Down

Sea Chantey

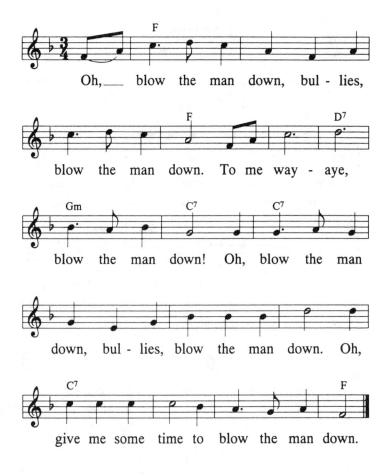

Oh,__ blow the man down, bul - lies,

blow the man down. To me way - aye,

blow the man down! Oh, blow the man

down, bul - lies, blow the man down. Oh,

give me some time to blow the man down.

Blow Ye Winds

Sea Chantey

'Tis ad - ver - tised in Bos - ton, New
York, and Buf - fa - lo, Five hun - dred brave A -
mer - i - cans, A - whal - ing for to go__, sing - ing

Chorus

Blow, ye winds, in the morn - ing,
Blow, ye winds, heigh - ho, Haul a - way your
run - ning gear, And blow, ye winds, heigh - ho.

Shenandoah
(Across the Wide Missouri)

Sea Chantey

1. Oh, Shen - an - doah, I long to hear you, Way,_ hay, you roll - ing riv - er! Oh, Shen - an - doah, I long to hear you, Way, hay, we're bound a - way, 'Cross the wide Mis - sour - i.

2. Oh, Shenandoah, I love your daughter,
   Way, hay, you rolling river,
   Oh, Shenandoah, I love your daughter,
   Way, hay, we're bound away,
   'Cross the wide Missouri.

3. Oh, Shenandoah, I love her truly,
   Way, hay you rolling river,
   Oh, Shenandoah, I love her truly,
   Way, hay, we're bound away,
   'Cross the wide Missouri.

4. I long to see your fertile valley,
   Way, hay you rolling river,
   I long to see your fertile valley,
   Way, hay, we're bound away,
   'Cross the wide Missouri.

5. Oh, Shenandoah, I'm bound to leave you,
   Way, hay you rolling river,
   Oh, Shenandoah, I'm bound to leave you,
   Way, hay, we're bound away,
   'Cross the wide Missouri.

Alouette

French Canadian

A - lou - et - te, gen - tille a - lou - et - te,

A - lou - et - te, je te plu - me - rai.

Je te plu - me - rai la tete,
Je te plu - me - rai le bec,

Je te plu - me - rai la tete,
Je te plu - me - rai le bec,

Et la tete, Et la tete. Oh!

Je te plumerai: (I will pluck your)
1. La tete (head)
2. Le bec (beak)
3. Le nez (nose)
4. Le dos (back)
5. Les pattes (feet)
6. Le cou (neck)

The Ash Grove

Welsh Folk Song

The ash grove, how__ grace - ful, how
Where - ev - er the____ light through its

plain - ly___ 'tis___ speak - ing, The
bran - ches_ is____ break - ing, I

harp through____ it_____ play - ing has
see the_____ kind__ fa - ces of

lan - guage for me; The_____
friends dear to me.

friends of_ my_ child - hood a - gain are_ be_-

fore me, Each step brings____ a__

139

mem - ory as free - ly I roam; With soft whis - pers___ speak - ing, its leaves rus___ - tle___ near me. The ash grove,_____ the___ ash grove a - lone is my home.

Au Clair de la Lune

French Folk Song

In the eve - ning moon - light,

My good friend Pier - rot, Please give me your

quill pen, Just to write a note.

For my can - dle's out now,

And my fire's out, too; O - pen your front

door, please, May I beg of you!

Au clair de la lune, Mon ami, Pierrot,
Prê-te-moi ta plume, Pour écríve un mot.
Ma chandelle est morte, Je n'ai plus de feu;
Ouvre-moi ta porte, Pour l'amour de Dieu!

2. Ladies, too, do like this, then again do like that.

3. Soldiers, too, do like this, then again do like that.

4. Children, too, do like this, then again do like that.

Sur le pont d'Avignon l'on y danse, l'on y danse,

Sur le pont d'Avignon l'on y danse tout en rond.

1. Les messieurs font comme çi, et puis encore comme ça.

2. Les dames font comme çi, et puis encore comme ça.

3. Les soldats font comme çi, et puis encore comme ça.

4. Les gamins font comme çi, et puis encore comme ça.

Auld Lang Syne

Robert Burruns

Scotland

1. Should auld ac - quaint - ance

be for - got, And nev - er brought to

mind? Should auld ac - quaint - ance

be for - got, And days of auld lang

syne? For auld___ lang___

syne, my dear, For auld___ lang___

syne; We'll take a cup of

kind - ness yet for auld___ lang___ syne.

2. We twa ha'e ran aboot the braes,
   And pu'd the gowans fine,
   We're wander'd mony a weary foot
   Sin auld lang syne. *(Chorus)*

3. We twa ha'e sported i' the burn
   Frae mornin' sun till dine,
   But seas between us brain ha'e roared
   Sin auld lang syne. *(Chorus)*

4. And here's a hand, my trusty friend,
   And gie's a hand of thine;
   We'll take a cup of kindness yet
   For auld lang syne. *(Chorus)*

Billy Boy

England

1. Oh,_____ where have you been, Bil - ly

Boy, Bil - ly Boy, Oh__ where have you

been, charm - ing Bil - ly?_____ I have

been to see my wife, she's the joy__ of my

life, She's a young thing and

can - not leave her moth - er._____

2. Did she bid you to come in, Billy Boy, Billy Boy,
   Did she bid you to come in, charming Billy?
   Yes, she bade me to come in, there's a dimple in her chin,
   She's a young thing and cannot leave her mother.

3. Can she make a cherry pie, Billy Boy, Billy Boy,
   Can she make a cherry pie, charming Billy?
   She can make a cherry pie, quick's a cat can wink her eye,
   She's a young thing and cannot leave her mother.

4. How old is she, Billy Boy, Billy Boy,
   How old is she, charming Billy?
   She's three times six, four times seven,
       twenty-eight and eleven,
   She's a young thing and cannot leave her mother.

The Bridge of Avignon
(Sur le Pont d'Avignon)

France

Chorus

On the bridge (of) A - vi - gnon

There is danc - ing, there is danc - ing,

On the bridge (of) A - vi - gnon

there is danc - ing all a - round.

Verse

1. Gen - tle - men do like this,

then a - gain do like that.

2. Ladies, too, do like this, then again do like that.

3. Soldiers, too, do like this, then again do like that.

4. Children, too, do like this, then again do like that.

Sur le pont d'Avignon I'on y danse, I'on y danse,

Sur le pont d'Avignon I'on y danse tout en rond.

1. Les messieurs font comme ci, et puis encore comme ca.

2. Les dames font comme ci, et puis encore comme ca.

3. Les soldats font comme ci, et puis encore comme ca.

4. Les gamins font comme ci, et puis encore comme ca.

The Children's Prayer

Words and music by
Engelbert Humperdinck

England

When at night I go to sleep, Four - teen an - gels

watch do _ keep; Two my head are guard - ing,

Two my feet are guid - _ ing, Two are on my

right hand, Two are on my left hand,

Two who warm - ly cov - er, Two who o'er me

hov - er, Two to whom 'tis giv - _ en To

light my way to Heav - _____ en.

Cielito Lindo
(Beautiful Heaven)

Mexico

1. From Sier - ra Mo - re - na, Cie - li - to
Lin - do, comes__ soft - ly steal - ing,__
Laugh-ing eyes,__ black and ro - guish, Cie
- li - to Lin - do, beau - ty re -
veal - ing.__ Ay, ay, ay,
ay!__ Sing,
ban - ish sor - row!__ To

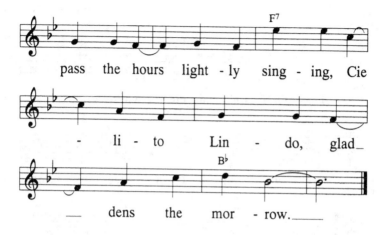

pass the hours light-ly sing-ing, Cie-li-to Lin-do, glad-dens the mor-row.

2. In the air brightly flashing,
   Cielito Lindo, flies Cupid's feather,
   My heart it is striking,
   Cielito Lindo, wounding forever.

1. De la Siera Morena, Cielito Lindo, vienen bajando;
   Un parde ojitos negros, Cielito Lindo, de contrabando.

   Chorus: ¡Ay, ay, ay, ay! Canta y no llores,
            Porque cantando se alegran, Cielito Lindo
            los corazones.

2. Una flecha en aire, Cielito Lindo, lanzo Cupido.
   Y como fue jugando, Cielito Lindo, yo fui el herido.

Cockles and Mussels

Irish Folk Song

1. In Dub - lin's fair cit - y, where girls are so

pret - ty, I first set my eyes on sweet

Mol - ly Ma - lone, As she wheeled her wheel -

bar - row through streets broad and

nar - row, Cry - ing "Cock - les and mus - sels, A-

live, a - live oh!" A - live, a - live

oh! ___ A - live, a - live oh! ___ Cry - ing

"Cock - les and mus - sels, a - live, a - live oh!"

2. She was a fishmonger, but sure, 'twas no wonder,
   For so were her father and mother before;
   And they wheeled their wheelbarrow
   through streets broad and narrow,
   Crying "Cockles and mussels, alive, alive oh!"
                                    (Refrain)

3. She died of a fever and no one could save her,
   And that was the end of sweet Molly Malone;
   Now her ghost wheels her barrow
   through streets broad an narrow,
   Crying "Cockles and mussels, alive, alive oh!"
                                    (Refrain)

Frog Went A-Courting

England

2. He rode right to Miss Mousie's door, uh, huh!
   He rode right to Miss Mousie's door, uh, huh!
   He rode right to Miss Mousie's door
   Where he had often gone before, uh, huh!

3. He took Miss Mousie on his knee,
   Said, "Miss Mousie, will you marry me?"uh, huh!, etc.

4. "Without my Uncle Rat's consent
   I couldn't marry the president!" uh, huh!, etc.

5. Uncle Rat gave his consent,
   So they got married an off they went, uh, huh!, etc.

6. Now, where will the wedding supper be?
   Away down yonder by the hollow tree, uh, huh!, etc.

7. Who's going to make the wedding gown?
   Old Miss Toad from the lily pond, uh, huh!, etc.

8. Now, what will the wedding supper be?
   Two big green peas and a black-eyed pea, uh, huh! etc.

9. Now, the first to come was a big white moth,
   She spread down a white table cloth, uh, huh! etc.

10. If you want this song again to ring,
    Make it up yourself and start to sing, uh, huh! etc.

Greensleeves
(What Child Is This)

England

1. A -las, my love,__ you do me wrong,__ To

cast me off__ dis - court - eous - ly And

I have loved__ you for so long,__ De -

light - ing in__ your com - pan - y.

Refrain

Green - sleeves__ was all my joy,__

Green__ - sleeves__ was my de - light,

Green- sleeves was my heart of gold,__ And

who but my lad___ - y Green - sleeves.

2. I long have waited at your hand
   To do your bidding as your slave,
   And waged, have I, both life and land
   Your love and affection for to have. *(Refrain)*

3. If you intend thus to disdain
   It does the more enrapture me,
   And even so, I will remain
   Your lover in captivity. *(Refrain)*

4. Alas, my love, that yours should be
   A heart of faithless vanity,
   So here I meditate alone
   Upon your insincerity. *(Refrain)*

5. Ah, Greensleeves, now farewell, adieu,
   To God I pray to prosper thee,
   For I remain thy lover true,
   Come once again and be with me. *(Refrain)*

Kumbayah

African Folk Song

Chorus
C
Kum - ba - yah, my Lord, ____

F   C
kum - ba - yah, ____

Kum - ba - yah, my Lord, ____

G⁷
kum - ba - yah, ____

C
____ Kum - ba - yah, my

F
Lord ____ kum - ba -

158

yah,

Oh, Lord,

kum - ba - yah.

1. Someone's singing, Lord, kumbayah, etc. *(Chorus)*

2. Someone's weeping, Lord, kumbayah, etc. *(Chorus)*

3. Someone's dancing, Lord, kumbayah, etc. *(Chorus)*

4. Someone's praying, Lord, kumbaya, etc. *(Chorus)*

Lavender's Blue

England

1. Lav - en - der's blue, dil - ly, dil - ly,

lav - en - der's green,

When I am king, dil - ly, dil - ly,

you shall be queen.

Who told you so, dil - ly, dil - ly, who told you so?

'Twas mine own heart, dil - ly, dil - ly,

that told me so.

Loch Lomond

Scotland

1. By＿ yon bon - nie banks and by

yon bon - nie braes, Where the

sun shines bright on Loch Lo - mond, Where

me and my true love were

ev - er wont to gae, On the

bon - nie, bon - nie banks of Loch Lo - mond.

Refrain

Oh! ye'll take the high road, and

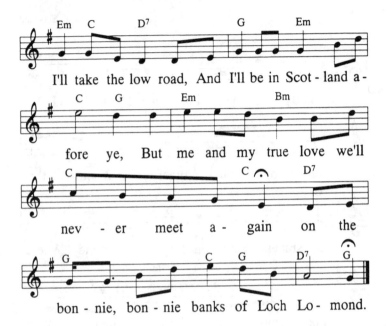

I'll take the low road, And I'll be in Scot - land a -
fore ye, But me and my true love we'll
nev - er meet a - gain on the
bon - nie, bon - nie banks of Loch Lo - mond.

2. 'Twas there that we parted in yon shady glen
On the steep, steep side of Ben Lomond,
Where in purple hue the highland hills we view,
And the moon coming out in the gloaming.
(Refrain)

3. The wee birdies sing, and the wild flowers spring,
And in sunshine the waters are sleeping,
But the broken hearts kens nae second spring again,
Though the waeful may cease frae their greeting.
(Refrain)

Lullaby

Johannes Brahms

2. Lullaby and goodnight, thy mother's delight,
   Bright angels beside my darling abide.
   They will guard thee at rest, thou shalt wake on my breast,
   They will guard thee at rest, thou shalt wake on my breast.

1. Guten Abend, gut' Nacht, mit Rosen bedacht,
   Mit Naglein besteckt, schlupf unter die Deck.
   Morgen fruh, wenn Gott will wirst du weider geweckt;
   Morgen fruh, wenn Gott will wirst du weider geweckt.

Mary Ann

Calypso Song

All night, all day, Miss Ma-ry Ann,

Down by the sea - side, sift - ing sand.

Ev - ery - bod -y down there join the band,

Down by the sea - side sift - ing sand.

Verse
If you come to our Port of Spain, you'll

nev - er want to go home a - gain.

You'll do ev - er - y - thing you can,

Just to be round Miss Ma - ry Ann.

Paper of Pins

British Isles

(Boys) I'll give to you a
(Girls) I'll not ac - cept your

pa - per of pins, And that's the way true
pa - per of pins, If that's the way your

love be - gins, if you will mar - ry
love be - gins, And I'll not mar - ry

me, me, me, If you will mar - ry me.
you, you, you, And I'll not mar - ry you.

2. I'll give to you a satin gown with silken
        tassels all around,
    If you will marry me, me, me, if you will marry me.
    I'll not accept your satin gown with silken
        tassels all around,
    And I'll not marry you, you, you, and I'll not marry you.

3. I'll give to you a dress of red all sewn
        around with golden thread
    If you will marry me, me, me, if you will marry me.
    I'll not accept your dress of red all sewn
        around with golden thread
    And I'll not marry you, you, you, and I'll not marry you.

4. I'll give to you my big black horse that's paced
        the meadow all across,
    If you will marry me, me, me, if you will marry me.
    I'll not accept your big black horse that's paced
        the meadow all across,
    And I'll not marry you, you, you, and I'll not marry you.

5. I'll give to you my hand and heart that you
        and I may never part,
    If you will marry me, me, me, if you will marry me.
    I'll not accept your hand and heart that you
        and I may never part,
    And I'll not marry you, you, you, and I'll not marry you.

6. I'll give to you a house and land, a William goat,
        A hired hand,
    If you will marry me, me, me, if you will marry me.

I'll not accept your house and land, your William goat,
   your hired hand,
And I'll not marry you, you, you, and I'll not marry you.

7. I'll give to you the key to my chest with gold
      whenever you request,
   If you will marry me, me, me, if you will marry me.
   I'll not accept the key to your chest with gold
      whenever I request,
   And I'll not marry you, you, you, and I'll not marry you.

8. O, now I see that money is king and your life
      didn't mean a thing,
   So I won't marry you, you, you, so I won't marry you.
   An old maid, then, I'll have to be, another I won't
      wed, you see,
   So won't you marry me, me, me, so won't you
      marry me?

Pop! Goes the Weasel

England

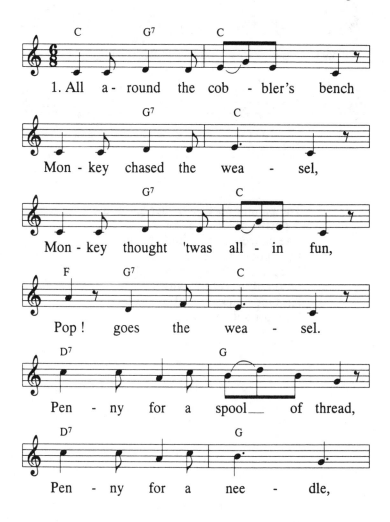

1. All a - round the cob - bler's bench

Mon - key chased the wea - sel,

Mon - key thought 'twas all - in fun,

Pop ! goes the wea - sel.

Pen - ny for a spool __ of thread,

Pen - ny for a nee - dle,

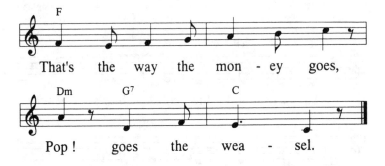

That's the way the mon - ey goes,

Pop ! goes the wea - sel.

2. The painter needs a ladder and brush,
   the artist needs an easel,
   The dancers need a fiddler's tune,
   Pop! goes the weasel;
   I've no time to wait or to sigh,
   or to tell the reason why,
   Kiss me quick, I'm off, good-by,
   Pop! goes the weasel.

Sarasponda

Dutch Spinning Song

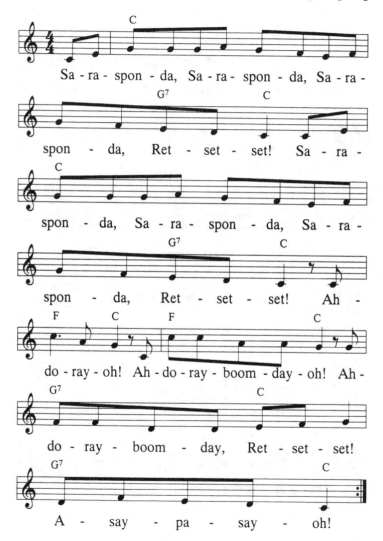

Sa - ra - spon - da, Sa - ra - spon - da, Sa - ra -
spon - da, Ret - set - set! Sa - ra -
spon - da, Sa - ra - spon - da, Sa - ra -
spon - da, Ret - set - set! Ah -
do - ray - oh! Ah - do - ray - boom - day - oh! Ah -
do - ray - boom - day, Ret - set - set!
A - say - pa - say - oh!

Scarborough Fair

English Folk Song

1. Are you go - ing to Scar - bor - ough
Fair?___ Pars - ley, sage, rose - mar - y and
thyme;___ Re -
mem - ber me to one that lives
there,___ For
she was once a true love of mine.___

2. Tell her to make me a cambric shirt.
   Parsley, sage, rosemary and thyme;
   Without a seam or fine needle work,
   And then she'll be a true love of mine.

3. Tell her to wash it in yonder dry well,
   Parsley, sage, rosemary and thyme;
   Where water ne'er sprung, nor drop of rain fell,
   And then she'll be a true love of mine.

4. Tell her to dry it on yonder thorn,
   Parsley, sage, rosemary and thyme;
   Which never bore blossom since Adam was born,
   And then she'll be a true love of mine.

5. Tell him to find me an acre of land,
   Parsley, sage, rosemary and thyme;
   Between the sea foam and the sea sand,
   Or never be a true love of mine.

6. Tell him to plough it with a lam'b horn,
   Parsley, sage, rosemary and thyme;
   And sow it all over with one peppercorn,
   Or never be a true love of mine.

7. Tell him to reap it with a sickle of leather,
   Parsley, sage, rosemary and thyme;
   And tie it all up with a peacock's feather,
   Or never be a true love of mine.

8. When he has done and finished his work,
   Parsley, sage, rosemary and thyme;
   Then come to me for his cambric shirt,
   And he shall be a true love of mine.

The More We Get Together

German Folk Melody

This Old Man

England

1. This old man, he played one,
He played nick-nack on my thumb, With a
nick-nack pad-dy whack give the dog a bone!
This old man came roll-ing home.

2. This old man, he played two,
   He played nick-nack on my shoe.

3. This old man, he played three,
   He played nick-nack on my knee.

4. This old man, he played four,
   He played nick-nack on my door.

5. This old man, he played five,
   He played nick-nack on my hive.

6. This old man, he played six,
   He played nick-nack on my sticks.

7. This old man, he played sev'n,
   He played nick-nack till elev'n.

8. This old man, he played eight,
   He played nick-nack on my gate.

9. This old man, he played nine,
   He played nick-nack on my spine.

10. This old man, he played ten,
    He played nick-nack over again.

Vesper Hymn

Russia

1. Hark! the ves - per hymn is steal - ing,
o'er the wa - ters soft and clear; Near -er yet and
near - er peal - ing, soft it breaks up -
on the ear. Ju - bi - la - te! Ju - bi - la - te!
Ju - bi - la - te! A___ - men.
Far - ther now and far - ther steal - ing,
soft it fades up___ - on the ear.

2. Now like moonlight waves retreating, to the
      shore it dies along;
   Now like angry surges meeting, breaks the
      mingled tide of song.
   Jubilate! Jubilate! Jubilate! Amen;
   Jubilate! Jubilate! Jubilate! Amen.
   Hark! Again like waves retreating, to the shore
      it dies along.

3. Once again sweet voices ringing, louder still
      the music swells;
   While on summer breezes winging, comes the
      chime of vesper bells.
   Jubilate! Jubilate! Jubilate! Amen;
   Jubilate! Jubilate! Jubilate! Amen.
   On the summer breezes winging, fades the chime
      of vesper bells.

We Gather Together

English Words by
Theodore Baker

Traditional Dutch Tune

1. We gath - er to - geth - er to ask the Lord's bless - ing; He chas - tens and has - tens His will to make known. The wick - ed op - press - ing, now cease____ from dis - tress - ing. Sing prais - es to His name; He for -

gets   not   His   own.

2. Beside us to guide us, our God with us joining,
   Ordaining, maintaining His kingdom divine.
   So from the beginning, the fight we were winning.
   Thou, Lord, wast at our side;
   All glory be thine.

3. We all do extol Thee, Thou leader triumphant,
   And pray that Thou still our defender wilt be.
   Let Thy congregation escape tribulation.
   Thy name be ever praised!
   O Lord, make us free!

Where Has My Little Dog Gone ?
(Der Deitcher's Dog)

Septimus Winner   Germany

Oh where, oh where has my lit - tle dog gone? Oh where, oh where can he be?___ With his tail cut short and his ears cut long, oh where, oh where can he be?___

Zum Gali Gali

Israeli Work Song

Chorus

Zum ga - li, ga - li, ga - li, Zum ga - li, ga - li

1. Pi - o - neers must work ev - 'ry day,
2. Pi - o - neers will sing and dance,
3. Pi - o - neers will work for peace,

From dawn 'til day is done;
Dance the ho - ra in a ring;
From dawn 'til day is done;

From dawn 'til day is done,
Dance the ho - ra in a ring,
From dawn 'til day is done,

There is work for ev - 'ry - one.
With their best gifts, dance and sing.
True peace for ev - 'ry - one.

Hebrew Transliteration:

He-kha-lutz le-maan a-v-dah;
A-vo-dah le-maan he-kha-lutz.
A-vo-dah le-maan he-kha-lutz;
He-kha-lutz le-maan a-vo-dah.

America

Samual Francis Smith

Henry Carey

2. My native country, Thee,
   land of the noble free, Thy name I love.
   I love Thy rocks and hills, thy woods and templed hills,
   My heart with rapture thrills Like that above.

3. Let music swell the breeze,
   and ring from all the trees, Sweet freedom's song.
   Let mortal tongues awake, let all that breathe partake,
   Let rocks their silence break, The sound prolong.

4. Our fathers' God, to Thee,
   Author of liberty, To Thee we sing.
   Long may our land be bright with freedom's holy light,
   Protect us by Thy might, Great God, our King!

America the Beautiful

Katharine Lee Bates   Samuel A. Ward

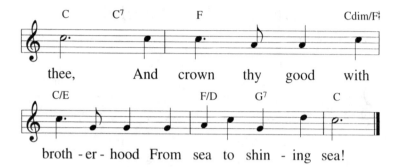

| C | C7 | F | | | Cdim/F♯ |

thee, And crown thy good with

| C/E | | | F/D | G7 | C |

broth - er - hood From sea to shin - ing sea!

2. O beautiful for Pilgrim feet,
   Whose stern impassioned stress
   A thoroughfare for freedom beat
   Across the wilderness.
   America! America! God mend thine every flaw,
   Confirm thy soul in self-control,
   Thy liberty in law.

3. O beautiful for heroes proved
   In liberating strife,
   Who more than self their country loved,
   And mercy more than life.
   America! America! May God thy gold refine
   Till all success be nobleness
   And every gain divine.

4. O beautiful for patriot dream
   That sees beyond the years,
   Thine alabaster cities gleam
   Undimmed by human tears.
   America! America! God shed His grace on thee,
   And crown thy good with brotherhood
   From sea to shining sea.

Battle Hymn of the Republic

Julia Ward Howe

William Steffe

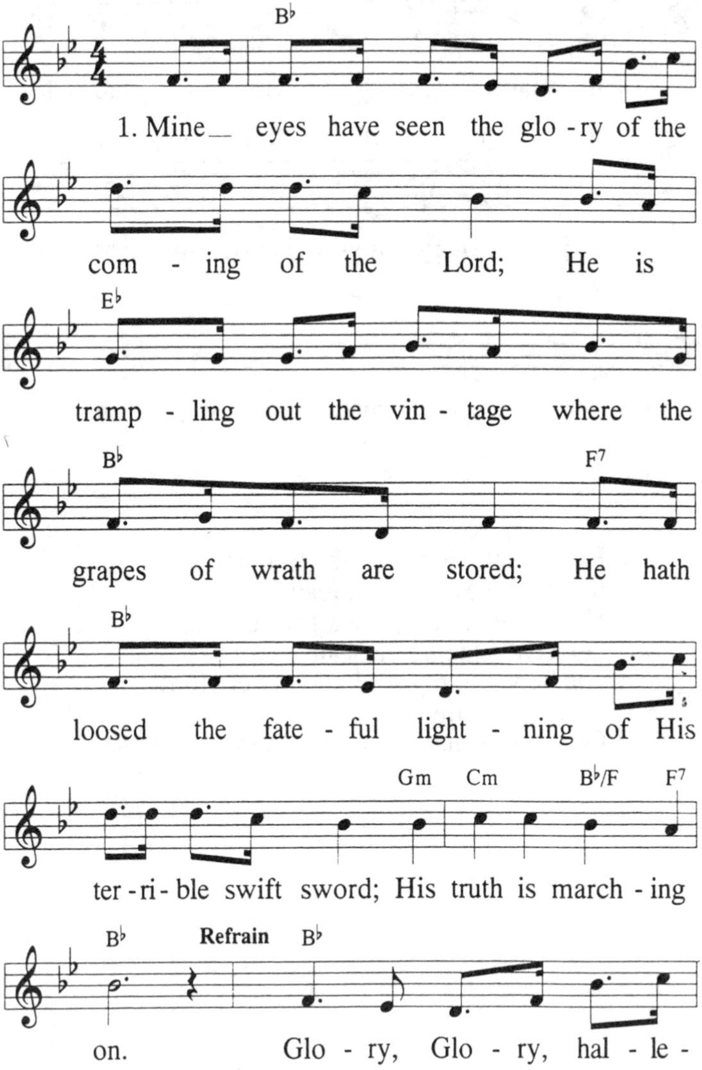

B♭
1. Mine__ eyes have seen the glo - ry of the
com - ing of the Lord; He is
E♭
tramp - ling out the vin - tage where the
B♭ F7
grapes of wrath are stored; He hath
B♭
loosed the fate - ful light - ning of His
Gm Cm B♭/F F7
ter - ri - ble swift sword; His truth is march - ing
B♭ Refrain B♭
on. Glo - ry, Glo - ry, hal - le -

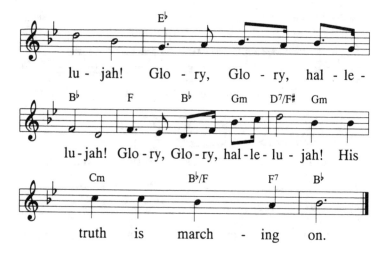

lu - jah! Glo - ry, Glo - ry, hal - le -
lu - jah! Glo - ry, Glo - ry, hal - le - lu - jah! His
truth is march - ing on.

2. He has sounded forth the trumpet
   that shall never call retreat;
   He is sifting out the hearts of men
   before the judgment seat.
   Oh, be swift, my soul, to answer Him!
   Be jubilant, my feet!
   Our God is marching on. *(Refrain)*

God of Our Fathers

George W. Warren

D.C. Roberts

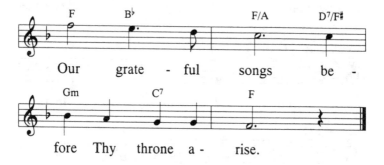

Our grate - ful songs be - fore Thy throne a - rise.

2. Thy love divine hath led us in the past,
   In this free land by Thee our lot is cast;
   Be Thou our Ruler, Guardian, Guide And Stay,
   Thy word our law, Thy paths our chosen way.

3. Refresh Thy people on their toilsome way,
   Lead us from night to never-ending day;
   Fill all our lives with love and grace divine,
   And glory, laud, and praise be ever Thine.

How Can I Keep From Singing?

Civil War Song

1. My life flows on in endless song,— above earth's lamentation.— I hear the real though far off hymn that hails a new creation.— No storm can shake my

2. Through all the tumult and the strife,— I hear that music ringing;— It sounds and echoes round me close, songs in the nights it sing-ing?— No storm can shake my

3. What, though the tempest round me 'rears,— I know the truth, it liveth.— What, though the dark-ness 'round me close, songs in the nights it giv-eth.— No storm can shake my

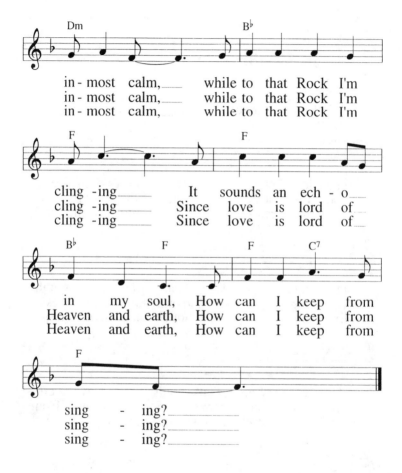